10/09

MY FIRST SPORTS

Baseball

by Ray McClellan

BELLWETHER MEDIA • MINNEAPOLIS, MN

Note to Librarians, Teachers, and Parents:

Blastoff! Readers are carefully developed by literacy experts and combine standards-based content with developmentally appropriate text.

Level 1 provides the most support through repetition of high-frequency words, light text, predictable sentence patterns, and strong visual support.

Level 2 offers early readers a bit more challenge through varied simple sentences, increased text load, and less repetition of high-frequency words.

Level 3 advances early-fluent readers toward fluency through increased text and concept load, less reliance on visuals, longer sentences, and more literary language.

Level 4 builds reading stamina by providing more text per page, increased use of punctuation, greater variation in sentence patterns, and increasingly challenging vocabulary.

Level 5 encourages children to move from "learning to read" to "reading to learn" by providing even more text, varied writing styles, and less familiar topics.

Whichever book is right for your reader, Blastoff! Readers are the perfect books to build confidence and encourage a love of reading that will last a lifetime!

This edition first published in 2010 by Bellwether Media, Inc.

No part of this publication may be reproduced in whole or in part without written permission of the publisher. For information regarding permission, write to Bellwether Media, Inc., Attention: Permissions Department, Post Office Box 19349, Minneapolis, MN 55419.

Library of Congress Cataloging-in-Publication Data

McClellan, Ray.
   Baseball / by Ray McClellan.
     p. cm. – (Blastoff! readers. My first sports)
   Includes bibliographical references and index.
   Summary: "Simple text and full color photographs introduce beginning readers to the sport of baseball. Developed by literacy experts for students in grades two through five"–Provided by publisher.
   ISBN 978-1-60014-277-2 (hardcover : alk. paper)
   1. Baseball–Juvenile literature. I. Title.

GV867.5.M395 2009
796.357–dc22

                              2009008157

Contents

What Is Baseball?

Baseball is one of the most popular sports in the world. Both kids and adults in several countries play it for fun. Many countries, such as Japan and the United States, also have professional leagues.

fun fact

Many people believe that an American named Abner Doubleday invented modern baseball in 1839. Others think Alexander Cartwright came up with the idea. He wrote the first baseball rule book in 1845.

cricket

Baseball was invented in the United States almost 200 years ago. It is thought to have grown out of games played in England. A ball is hit with a bat in games such as cricket, rounders, and stoolball.

In 1876, the National League formed with eight teams. In 1901, the American League formed with eight teams. It soon joined the National League. Baseball grew as more teams were added in more cities across the country.

The Basic Rules of Baseball

A baseball game lasts nine innings and is played by two teams. In the first half of an inning, the visiting team comes up to bat. When it makes three outs, its turn is over, and it is the home team's turn to bat.

There are several ways to make an out. A batter can get three **strikes** and strike out. A runner not on a base can be tagged out or forced out. Fielders can also catch balls hit into the air to make outs.

left fielder

center fielder

shortstop

second baseman

third baseman

pitcher

catcher

right fielder

first baseman

The team that is not at bat has nine players in the field. The **infield** includes the first baseman, second baseman, third baseman, and **shortstop**. The pitcher and catcher are also in the infield. The **outfield** includes the left fielder, center fielder, and right fielder.

The pitcher stands on the pitcher's mound and throws the ball to the catcher. The pitcher tries to get it inside the **strike zone**.

Batters get on base when they get a **hit**. A hit can be a single, double, triple, or **home run**. Batters can also take four **balls** to **walk** or get on base when a fielder makes an **error**.

fun fact

Little League Baseball was formed in Pennsylvania in 1939.

Every time a runner crosses home plate before three outs are made, a run is scored. The team that scores the most runs wins the game.

Baseball players need lots of equipment. Baseball bats can be made of metal or wood. In professional baseball, only wooden bats are used. Bats made of **aluminum** are common in college and Little League games.

! fun fact

Most baseballs are made with cork at the center. Yarn or twine is wrapped around the cork. A white leather cover goes around the ball. The cover is sewn on with red stitches.

Fielders need gloves. Baseball gloves are made of leather. There are many kinds of baseball gloves. A catcher's glove is large with extra padding to catch hard, fast pitches.

An infielder's glove is smaller. It is made so that an infielder can easily scoop up a ball and get the ball out to throw.

Hanley Ramirez

Today, baseball is very popular around the world. People of all ages love to play and watch the game. Stars such as Hanley Ramirez and Johan Santana continue to draw fans to Major League games.

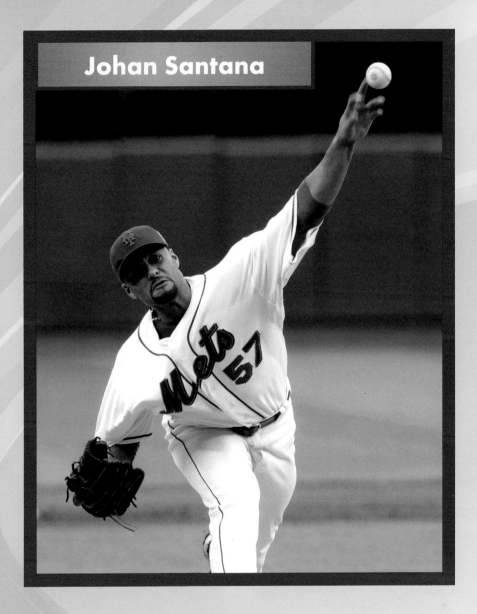

Johan Santana

Major League Baseball has 30 teams and is divided into two leagues. The American League has 14 teams. The National League has 16. Each league is split into three divisions.

In each league, the three division winners and one **wild card** team make the play-offs. The winner of each league goes to the **World Series**. At the World Series, the best team from each league battles for the championship.

Glossary

aluminum—a strong, lightweight metal used to make some baseball bats

ball—a pitch outside of the strike zone at which the batter does not swing

error—when a fielder drops a ball or throws it wildly and allows a runner to reach a base or move up a base

hit—when a batter reaches a base by hitting the ball into the field

home run—when a batter hits a ball and can run around all of the bases to score; most home runs go over the outfield fence.

infield—the area that includes the bases, pitcher's mound, and home plate

outfield—the area beyond the infield, farthest from home plate

shortstop—a fielder who usually plays between second base and third base

strike—a pitch that is in the strike zone or one that a player swings at and misses; a foul ball counts as a strike, but a player cannot strike out from one.

strike zone—the area from a hitter's knees to his chest that is directly over home plate

walk—when a batter takes first base after getting four balls

wild card—the team that has the most wins in each league of Major League Baseball but is not a division championship winner

World Series—the championship series of Major League Baseball featuring the winners of the American League and National League

To Learn More

AT THE LIBRARY

Craats, Rennay. *For the Love of Baseball*. New York, N.Y.: Weigl, 2003.

Doeden, Matt. *The Greatest Baseball Records*. Mankato, Minn.: Capstone, 2008.

Kelley, James. *Baseball*. New York, N.Y.: DK Publishing, 2005.

ON THE WEB

Learning more about baseball is as easy as 1, 2, 3.

1. Go to www.factsurfer.com.

2. Enter "baseball" into the search box.

3. Click the "Surf" button and you will see a list of related Web sites.

With factsurfer.com, finding more information is just a click away.

Index

The images in this book are reproduced through the courtesy of: Rob Friedman, front cover; Jim Kolaczko, pp. 4-5; Stuart Hannagan, p. 6; Mike Carlson / Associated Press, p. 7; Ronald Manera, p. 8; Gene J. Puskar / Associated Press, pp. 9, 13; MLB Photos via Getty Images, pp. 10-11, 14-15; Jim McIsaac / Getty Images, p. 12; Yellow Dog Productions / Getty Images, p. 16; Carolyn Kaster / Associated Press, p. 17; Joe Robbins / Getty Images, p. 18; Ed Betz / Associated Press, p. 19; Charles Krupa / Associated Press, pp. 20-21.